Ducks and Chicks

By Cameron Macintosh

Look at the ducks!

Ducks can be big.

They can be little, too.

This duck has chicks.

Her chicks are very little.

They have lots of fuzz!

fuzz

A duck can peck with its bill.

This duck has a long bill!

Ducks can dip to get little snacks.

The back end of the duck pops up!

Chicks can snack on bugs.

Big ducks can snack on fish.

But do not toss buns
to them!

A duck can swim very well.

It swims with its legs.

It kicks and kicks.

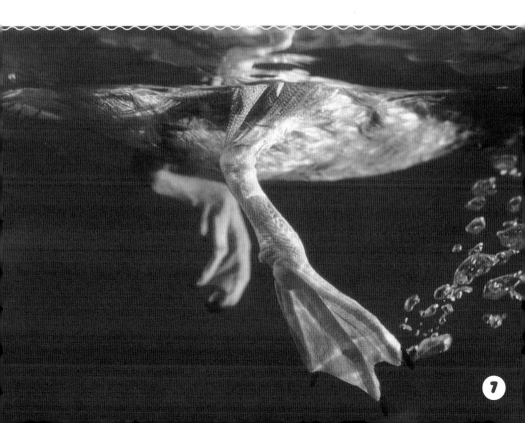

This duck sits on the rocks.

It tucks its bill in its wing when it naps.

See all the ducks
on the dock!

They can sit for a bit,
and then they will swim.

CHECKING FOR MEANING

1. What does a duck use to peck? *(Literal)*

2. How does a duck swim? *(Literal)*

3. Why do you think a duck tucks its bill under its wing when it sleeps? *(Inferential)*

EXTENDING VOCABULARY

fish	What is the sound at the end of this word? Make three lists of words you know with *sh–* at the start, the end and the middle. Ask a partner to read your word lists.
tucks	What are the sounds in this word? What does *tucks* mean? If you tuck your legs, what do you do with them?
wing	How many sounds are in this word? What are they? Can you change the first letter to make new words? E.g. ring, sing, bring, thing.

MOVING BEYOND THE TEXT

1. What are baby ducks sometimes called?

2. Why do ducklings have fuzz? Do ducks have fuzz?

3. Why is it important not to throw food to ducks?

4. Where can you see ducks near your home or school?

SPEED SOUNDS

sh	ch	th	th	ck	ng
		voiced	unvoiced		

PRACTICE WORDS

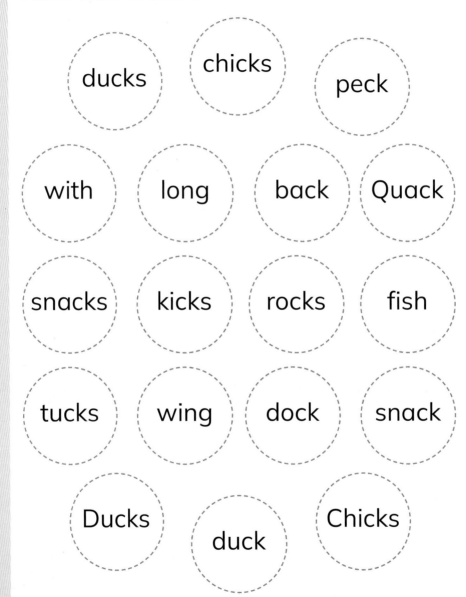

ducks

chicks

peck

with

long

back

Quack

snacks

kicks

rocks

fish

tucks

wing

dock

snack

Ducks

duck

Chicks